ALLEN COUNTY PUBLIC LIBRARY
3 1833 04950 2674

P9-CND-512

by Jen Jones

Mankato, Minnesota

Snap Books are published by Capstone Press,
151 Good Counsel Drive, P.O. Box 669, Mankato, Minnesota 56002
www.capstonepress.com

Printed in the United States of America

Library of Congress Cataloging-in-Publication Data
Jones, Jen, 1976-
Cheer basics: rules to cheer by / by Jen Jones.
p. cm. — (Snap books cheerleading)
Includes index.
ISBN 0-7368-4359-0 (hardcover)
1. Cheerleading — Juvenile literature. I. Title. II. Series.
LB3635.J62 2006
791.6'4 — dc22 2005007265

Summary: A guide for children and pre-teens on the basics of cheerleading.

Editor: Deb Berry/Bill SMITH STUDIO
Illustrators: Lisa Parett; Roxanne Daner, Marina Terletsky and Brock Waldron/Bill SMITH STUDIO
Designers: Marina Terletsky, and Brock Waldron/Bill SMITH STUDIO
Photo Researcher: Iris Wong/Bill SMITH STUDIO

Photo Credits: Cover: Tim Jackson Photography; 6, Bettmann/Corbis; 9, Joseph Sohm/ChromoSohm Inc./Corbis; 10, Peter Hvizdak/The Image Works; 22, EditorialFotos/Alamy; 28-29, Brooks Kraft/Corbis; 32, Britton Lenahan; Back Cover, Getty Images. All other photos by Tim Jackson Photography.

1 2 3 4 5 6 10 09 08 07 06 05

Table of Contents

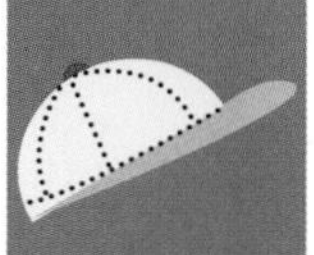

INTRODUCTION

Gimme A 'C-H-E-E-R'

Is being a fan in the stands just not enough? Are you ready to spur your team to victory? Cheerleading just might be right for you! Since 1898, cheerleaders have led crowds in rooting for their favorite sports teams. Through the years, elements like dance, gymnastics, and stunting have been added to the traditional yell-leading.

As a cheerleader, you'll represent your squad, your school, and your sports teams. The other kids at school will count on you to be a role model and entertainer. Oh, and did we mention cheerleading also requires top-notch athletic skills? The physical challenges of cheering demand well-rounded skills and a can-do attitude. And you *can* do it!

Cheerleading sets itself apart as one of the only year-round sports. It's an attitude, a lifestyle, and a pastime that is growing in popularity. Taking part in the sport leaves cheerleaders with lifetime leadership skills and unforgettable memories.

In this book, you'll learn about the background and basics of cheerleading. You'll receive lessons on all the "must-know" cheer skills: motions, jumps, cheering, and dancing.

"You can do it!"

So Much More Than Just "Rah, Rah, Rah"

The sport of cheerleading isn't new. It has been around for over 100 years! To learn your cheer history, take a timeline trip down memory lane.

1800s Princeton boasted the first pep club, but cheerleading officially started at the University of Minnesota. Student Johnny Campbell led crowds in the now-legendary yell, "Rah, rah, rah! Ski-U-Mah! Varsity, varsity, Minnesota!"

1900-1930 Progress! Women got permission to join previously all-male squads. Cheerleaders started using **megaphones**.

1948 Fifty-two cheerleaders attended the first cheerleading camp in Texas, organized by cheer pioneer Lawrence J. Herkimer.

1970-1990 Cheer, as we know it, took shape, adding dance, gymnastics, and stunting. National contests and cheer companies made cheerleading a true sport.

Present Cheerleading has worldwide reach and respect with more than 6 million cheerleaders in 38 countries. In the U.S., 80 percent of schools have at least one cheerleading team. All-star teams have also gained in popularity with 2,500 gyms across the nation.

It All Starts with a Smile!

Have you watched cheerleaders in action? They're yelling, moving, flipping, and dancing, often at the same time. It takes a lot of staying power to cheer without losing your breath. How do cheerleaders make it look so easy?

We'll tell you the big secret. Though practice and experience are obvious answers, it's as simple as . . . a smile!

Smiles are catching. The crowd relies on the squad's energy as their cue to get pumped up. While cheerleaders are entertainers, their main role is to spread school spirit at sports events. If the cheerleaders aren't having fun, how can anyone expect the crowd to be having fun? Spirit starts with you, and the easiest way to show it is by flashing those pearly whites.

Real excitement is the most important quality to have as a cheerleader. Whether you're cheering at a game or making a public appearance, let your smile shine through.

Cheer-Tionary

Before learning the moves of cheerleading, let's get familiar with common terms. That way, you talk just like one of the pros.

Wendy Wannabe Wonders,
What's the difference between . . .

A cheer and a chant? Repeated three times, a chant is a catchy set of sentences designed for crowd participation. Cheers are longer and often feature signs or stunting.

A clap and a clasp? Claps are tight with flat palms. Clasps are louder and stronger, with hands gripping each other. Both create rhythm and dramatic pauses in cheers.

◀ Clasp

Wendy Wannabe Wonders,
Are all cheer squads the same?

Far from it. Sports squads cheer on the sidelines, while competition squads focus on winning cheer competitions. All-star squads unite cheerleaders from different schools to compete together on a large athletic team. All three types can be either all-girl or a mix of boys *and* girls. Also in the cheer family are dance/drill teams and kick lines.

"Talk like one of the pros!"

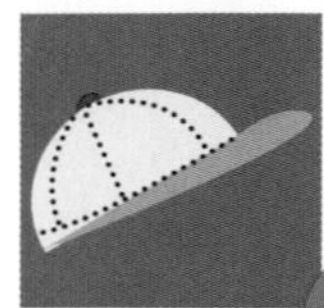

Wendy Wannabe Wonders, What on earth is . . .

A spirit stick? Spirit sticks are awarded at camp to the most eager and loyal cheerleaders. Legend has it that spirit sticks should never touch the ground, for fear of bad luck in competition.

A formation? "Formations" are shapes that show cheerleaders where to stand during routines, like a "V" or straight line. The coach decides placement by skill and height.

A peel-off? A "peel-off" is a visual effect. Remember the time your music teacher made you sing in rounds? It's a bit like that. All cheerleaders do the same movements at different times. The visual effect looks like a wave.

Wendy Wannabe Wonders, Gimme the skinny on stunting.

Partner stunts require a great deal of teamwork and strength. Popular stunts include pyramids, shoulder stands/sits, and **extensions**. **Flyers** stand atop the **mount**, while **bases** support their weight. Never attempt stunts without your coach present.

"Stunts require teamwork and strength."

Warm It Up, Everyone

Before you can fire up the crowd, you need to warm up your body! Stretching is a must before cheering at practices and games. Doing so reduces your chance of injury and makes you more flexible. Limber up with these common stretches.

Runner's Stretch In push-up position, bring right leg forward so that your foot is in front of your hands. Lean into the stretch without letting your knee go over your toes.

Balancing Act Stand and bend one leg behind you. Keep your knees close together and grab your raised foot just behind your, well, behind. Hold the pose. It's okay to use something (or someone) for balance. Repeat on opposite side.

Leg Spread Sit down and open your legs wide. Bending to one side, lower your head and arms toward your foot. Repeat on other side, then bend to the middle. Hold each position for 10 seconds.

◀ Leg Spread

Motions, The Building Blocks of Cheer

Motions fire up your words and create stunning visuals. Once you've mastered motions, you'll be well on your way to conquering just about any routine. Here are a few staples to set you in motion.

T Arms jut out from shoulders for a nifty "T" look. For "broken T," bend arms inward from T position.

L One arm is in "fight" and the other in "T" position.

Broken T

High V Arms form a "V" shape above your head with palms facing outward.

Low V Turn that "V" upside down. Now your body looks like a giant "M." (Who knew the alphabet came in so handy?)

Fight/Touchdown In fight position, one arm is above your head and the other hand is on your hip. For touchdown (or "double fight"), both arms go straight above head with fists facing.

Diagonal Put one arm in "high V" and the other in "low V." You've got a diagonal.

High V

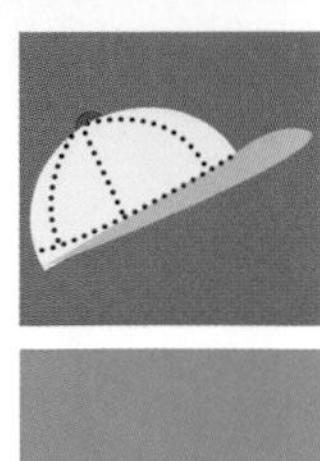

Now that you've grasped basic motions, it's time to nail down the nitty-gritty. All motions use one of two hand placements.

Fists For **candlesticks**, fists turn to the side, as if you're holding candles. In **buckets,** fists face down as if . . . you get the picture. For safety reasons, avoid tucking your thumb inside your fist.

▲ Candlesticks

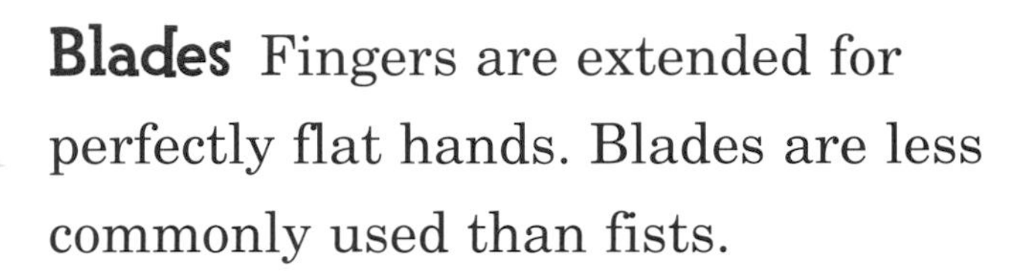

◀ Blades

Blades Fingers are extended for perfectly flat hands. Blades are less commonly used than fists.

If you think these motions sound easy, you're right. However, the real key to great motions is keeping movements sharp. Use your strength to hit each motion, but keep it controlled. There's nothing worse than a "Flyaway Fran!"

Helpful Hint Never overextend your arms behind you. You should normally be able to see both hands out of the corner of your eye.

Big No-No, Broken Wrists Never bend your wrists. Always keep arms in a straight line, whether in fists or blades.

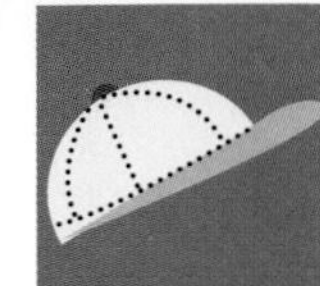

Jump to It

How do cheerleaders get so high off the ground doing toe touches, tucks, and herkies? These jumps may *look* easy, but in reality, touching those toes is harder than it looks. Your abs and legs must be in tip-top shape to lift your jumps upward.

Before any jump, a takeoff to a count of "8" is done as preparation. The toe touch is the most common jump. For a toe touch, you jump in the air, spread your legs, and touch your toes. But there are dozens of other jumps in cheering, too. Here are a few to get you off the ground.

Hurdler/Herkie Imagine a high kick with the other leg bent behind you. (Don't bend forward to meet your foot.) A herkie is similar, but to the side.

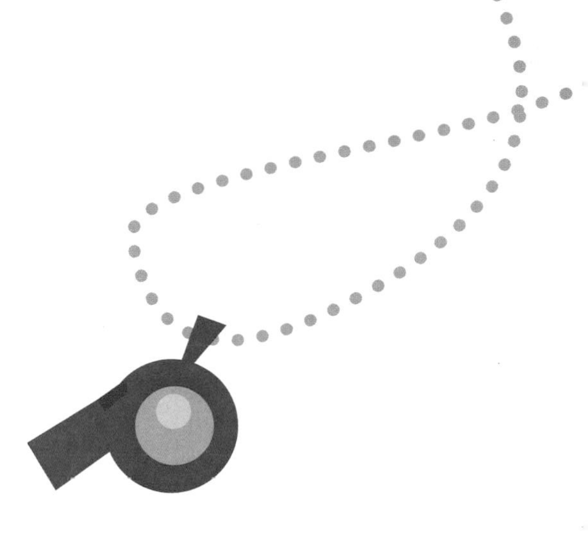

◀ Herkie

Pike A highly difficult jump, arms and legs are parallel in front of you.

Spread Eagle Arms are in a high V, while feet are in low V formation. Your body should look like an "X" in the air.

Sample Cheers and Chants

Now that you've got the basics down, let's put them in practice.

Tips to remember

- Yell in a loud, firm voice. No singing or high-pitched voices allowed!
- Don't rush it. You'll lose the crowd's interest and ability to follow along.
- Smile, stay focused, and keep motions sharp.
- Have fun!

General Chants

Who is the best?
S-M-S

Tigers X Get Tough
Show Us What You Got

Defense Chants

Sack That Quarterback
C'mon Defense X
Attack

Take It X Away
Big Green
Steal That Ball

Offense Chants

Touchdown X Tigers!
We Want a Win

The Hoop is Open
The Net is Hot
Make That Shot

Sample Cheers

Let's Go Tigers X
Fight, Fight, Fight X
Beat Those Pirates X
Win Tonight!

Tigers X
On 3, yell "Green"
1,2,3
GREEN!
Tigers X
On 3, yell "White"
1,2,3
WHITE!
All together,
let's hear you yell
GREEN AND WHITE!

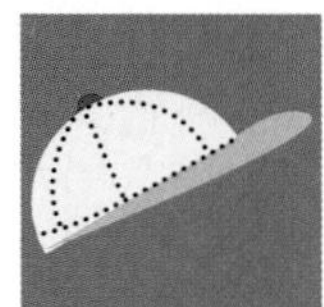

Everybody Dance Now

From peewee teams to the Laker Girls, cheer squads everywhere dazzle audiences with dance. Taught in "8-counts," routines can be up to three minutes long. Keep your dances from being duds with these hip tips.

Pick a catchy soundtrack to connect with the crowd Oldies are always a fun bet, while hip-hop gets the crowd jamming with you. Avoid naughty lyrics or slow tempos.

Play dress-up Jazz up your routine by using pom-poms or props. Funky accessories or costumes will also add flavor.

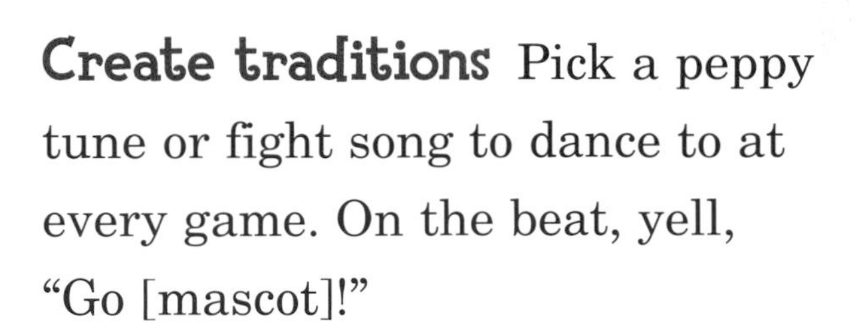

Create traditions Pick a peppy tune or fight song to dance to at every game. On the beat, yell, "Go [mascot]!"

Mix it up For surefire crowd-pleasers, sprinkle stunts, tumbling, or kick lines inside your routine.

Strike a pose Hold the ending pose for several seconds and let the effect sink in.

In Madonna's words,

"Get into the groove!"

Cheering Here, There, and Everywhere

Cheering here, there and everywhere. It rings like a Dr. Seuss poem, but it's what you can expect.

Unlike other sports, cheerleading is an all-year activity. After spring tryouts, you'll spend the summer bonding with your teammates and learning cheers and dance routines. Cheerleading camp is also a treasured summer tradition. For several days, you'll spend every waking moment cheering and having a blast! Don't stress about camp expenses, that's what fund-raisers are for.

After the hazy days of summer, it's back to school. A cheerleader's typical school year will include:

- Cheering at sports events
- Performing at pep rallies and events
- Cheerleading competitions
- Squad fund-raisers
- Weekly practices

Obviously, a cheerleader is always in motion. While you shouldn't have to give up other interests, cheerleading *does* take up a lot of time. Are you ready for it? If you say, "Bring it on," get ready for the time of your life!

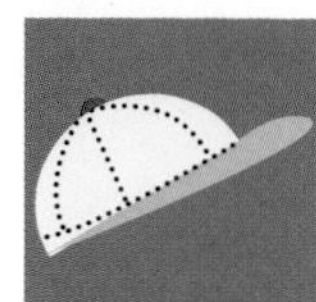

Spotlight On Famous Cheerleaders

Some of your favorite stars shouted on the sidelines before taking the stage. Find out which stars shook their pom-poms before rising to fame.

Christina Aguilera While growing up in Pennsylvania, Christina Aguilera got lots of practice wearing short skirts on her school's cheer squad.

George W. Bush President Bush prepared for his leadership role in the White House by leading crowds at Andover in Massachusetts.

Sandra Bullock The *Miss Congeniality* star perfected that movie-star smile on the sidelines.

Cameron Diaz Before life as one of *Charlie's Angels*, Cameron Diaz was *The Sweetest Thing* on her high school squad.

Kirsten Dunst It was no stretch for Kirsten Dunst to headline the cheer classic *Bring It On*!

Madonna The Material Girl was once, you guessed it, a Ma-Cheer-ial Girl.

Susan Lucci She might play the wicked Erica Kane on *All My Children,* but in real life, this soap opera star was once a sweet-as-pie cheerleader.

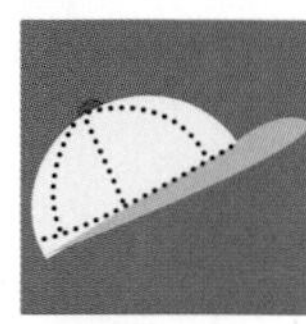

GLOSSARY

base (BAYSS) the person or people on the bottom of a mount

extension (ek-STEN-shuhn) two bases hold a flyer at chest level and extend their arms so that the flyer is above their heads

flexibility (FLEK-suh-buhl-i-tee) being able to bend and stretch without getting hurt

flyer (FLYER) a lightweight, very flexible person on top of a mount

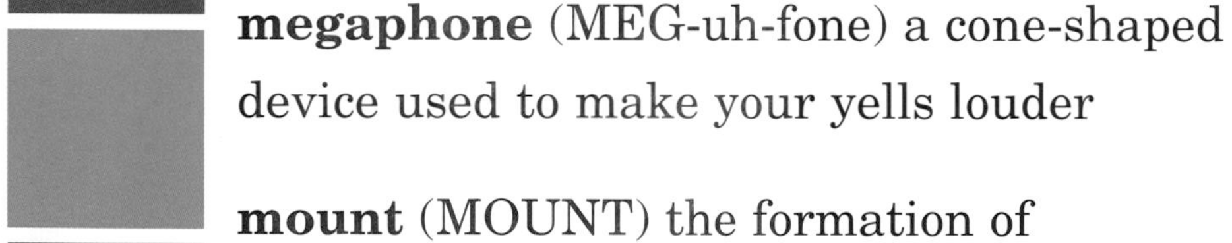

megaphone (MEG-uh-fone) a cone-shaped device used to make your yells louder

mount (MOUNT) the formation of cheerleaders sitting or standing on top of one another

partner stunt (PART-nur STUHNT) cheerleaders standing or sitting on top of one another, also known as a "mount," or as a "pyramid" when several stunts are shown as a group

FAST FACTS

Smart Cookies

Eighty-three percent of all cheerleaders have a "B" grade-point average or better.

The Birth of Poms

In 1965, Fred Gastoff invented the first vinyl pom-pom. One small step for mankind, one giant step for cheerkind!

Cheer in the U.S.A.

In the United States, there are more than 3 million Pop Warner, high school and college cheerleaders. The number is growing by the minute.

Gimme an "Ouch"

Among the most common cheerleading injuries are split lips and ankle sprains.

I Scream, You Scream, We All Scream for Pigskin

Football is the most common sport for cheerleading.

READ MORE

Golden, Suzi J. and Roger Schreiber. *101 Best Cheers: How to Be the Best Cheerleader Ever*. New York: Troll Communications, 2001.

McElroy, James T. *We've Got Spirit: The Life and Times of America's Greatest Cheerleading Team*. New York: Berkley Publishing Group, 2000.

Neil, Randy and Elaine Hart. *The Official Cheerleader's Handbook*. New York: Fireside, 1986.

Peters, Craig. *Competitive Cheerleading*. Broomall, Pennsylvania: Mason Crest, 2003.

Wilson, Leslie. *The Ultimate Guide to Cheerleading*. New York: Three Rivers Press, 2003.

INTERNET SITES

FactHound offers a safe, fun way to find Internet sites related to this book. All of the sites on FactHound have been researched by our staff.

Here's how

1. Visit *www.facthound.com*

2. Type in this special code **0736843590** for age-appropriate sites. Or enter a search word related to this book for a more general search.

3. Click on the **Fetch It** button.

FactHound will fetch the best sites for you!

ABOUT THE AUTHOR

While growing up in Ohio, Jen Jones spent seven years as a cheerleader for her grade-school and high-school squads. Following high school, she coached several cheer squads to team victory. For two years, she also cheered and created dance numbers for the Chicago Lawmen semi-professional football dance team.

Jen gets her love of cheerleading honestly, because her mother, sister, and cousins are also heavily involved in the sport. As well as teaching occasional dance and cheerleading workshops, Jen now works in sunny Los Angeles as a freelance writer for publications like *American Cheerleader* and *Dance Spirit.*

Index